How to Design a Kindle eBook Cover

Revised Edition 3

How to For You Series #8

Dorothy May Mercer

Published in the United States by

© 2014, 2015, 2019 Mercer Publications

& Ministries, Inc.

Stanwood, Michigan 49346

ISBN 13:978-1-62329-087-0

ISBN 10: 1-62329-087-2

Publisher: Mercer Publications

& Ministries, Inc.

Stanwood, Michigan 49346

TABLE OF CONTENTS

Introduction 5

Why Design Your Own Cover?...................................5

Amazon's Cover Creator Software 5

Opening Kindle Cover Creator 6

Working With "1 Choose Design" 9

Using Your Own Image 10
Purchasing a Licensed Picture 10

Working with "2 Style and Edit."........................... 14

Working with Layout 16
Working with Design Elements 16

Working with "3 Preview" 18

Save and Submit 22

Buying a License for a Picture 23

Dear Reader **27**

Two easy ways... 29

<u>**The complete "How to For You" series of booklets for**</u>
<u>**improving writers and Indie Publishers.**</u> **30**

BOOKS FROM MERCER PUBLICATIONS **32**

Introduction

Why Design Your Own Cover?

So you have written the great American novel and now you are an impoverished "Indie Publisher."

Like the rest of us, you are trying to get your eBook "out there." But, costs are mounting up. It's true—all the advisors recommend you buy a good cover. However, you have priced the service of a good professional cover designer. Frightening, isn't it?

Not to mention, editing, formatting, proof-reading and marketing assistance. Oh my goodness!

Ka-Ching, ka-ching!

Well, take heart, my friend. For the investment of mere pennies, plus your time, I will tell you how to make your own cover. And then, if you do not like the results, you can always hire the professional, later. Even if you throw away your creation, you will have learned a few tricks. It will be fun, too.

Amazon's Cover Creator Software

Amazon, bless their hearts, have provided you with all you need to get going on this project, for free.

Note: You can buy cover design software, for one hundred bucks, and up, if you are a reasonably good artist, but it is not for we amateurs. No offense.

Moving on... Kindle Cover Creator is user friendly, but this article will hasten your learning process, and hopefully, teach you are few tricks and shortcuts and save you from a few mistakes, like losing all your work because you forgot to Save. Can it get any worse than that?

For our purposes, we will assume that you have already mastered the interior of your eBook, and you think you can recognize a pretty good cover when you see one. (See my book, "How to Prepare Your Book for Kindle" and others.) So, now you are ready to design the cover.

Opening Kindle Cover Creator

First, open a https://kdp.amazon.com/en US/ account, enter your ID and password and click "Sign In." (Other countries will leave off the en.US.)

Perhaps you have already begun the entry file for your book. If so, simply click on the yellow button to "Continue Setup." (If that is not available open the menu at the right which is located under the three tiny dots. Simply hover your mouse and a menu will open.)

If you have not begun a file, click a plus sign under "Create New Title." You will be taken to a new page, Kindle eBook Details, where you can enter all the details for your eBook.

Notice the three headers: Kindle ebook Details, Kindle eBook Content and Kindle eBook Pricing

Note: A word of caution: At the bottom of the page are two important choices:

- Save and Continue.
- Save as Draft.

So long as you are in the process, be sure and click one of these choices whenever you exit a page. Do not use the back arrow to exit. Otherwise, you will lose any new entries. "Save As Draft" will safely return you to your Bookshelf. Use "Save and Continue" when you are ready to move on to the next page.

There will be times when the program will refuse to let you save and continue. That is because there are certain items which must be filled in first. These will be indicated in red. Go back and make entries in these fields. Most, not all, of them can be changed later.

For now, fill in your working title, your author name, description, publishing rights, catagories and pre-order date. You can finish the rest later and you can change this date, as well, to an earlier date, but not later.

Click Save and Continue. This takes you to the "Kindle eBook Content" page.

Scroll down to "Kindle eBook Cover."

> (Note: If you already have a printed book cover, you can edit that cover using "crop" and then "upload" the front page, but for the purposes of this section, we will assume you are starting from scratch.)

Choose "Launch Cover Creator."

Choose "Continue."

The first page, How to Use Cover Creator, is just of your information. You will note three sections.

> 1. Choose a Design
> 2. Style and Edit
> 3. Preview

Later you can toggle back and forth between these three work areas. For now, click "Continue."

The next page, "Get images for your cover" gives you three choices. Do you have an image in mind? Either upload it, choose one from their free image gallery or skip this step, for now. You may either add an image later or choose a design which uses no image.

The first of three pages, "Choose Design", opens. Your author and title information will be displayed on a selection of covers, some with images, some not.

You can toggle back and forth among the three headings, Choose Design, Style & Edit, and Preview. Of course, the handy Undo button is there, as well.

Working With "1 Choose Design"

For now we will stay in "1 Choose Design" and play around with this for a while. You are aiming to choose a basic layout and background. Later we will fiddle with colors and fonts.

While in "1 Choose Design," click on any cover selection. Notice you have suddenly moved to section "2 Syle & Edit." Move your mouse around on this cover and notice the commands that pop up. Select "Click to Edit or Change Image." Do not worry about making a mistake. Everything can be changed. Spend some time here, trying out all sorts of images and backgrounds. Start by opening, "From the gallery." Find one you wish to try and click "Use this image." Suddenly the image pops into your design. Click the "Choose Design" heading and you will see your choice of pictures is now up on some of the book designs.

(Note: Some of the layouts are Non-image designs.)

Repeat the process, try another and another. There are hundreds of choices, all free for your use. You are looking for an image that, more or less, gives the customer a clue as to what this book is about, and also screams, "Look at me, look at me," no matter whether it is full size or thumbnail size.

Using Your Own Image

Maybe you simply cannot find a free one that works. In this case, after you select "Choose a new cover image," click "From my computer." Make sure that you own all the rights to any image you use from your own computer.

If you use a picture that you have taken yourself, you are all right, unless it is a picture of another person, or another entity's private possession, or a patented, copyrighted or trademarked item. Examine your picture to make certain no trademarked or patented logo shows, not even a Coca-cola sign.(Example: Disney World.) In such a case you would need that person or entity's written release to actually publish it. However, there are no restrictions on trying it out, at this point. (Well, I do not need to add "avoid porno, or offensive pictures," do I?)

Purchasing a Licensed Picture

You may still be dissatisfied. Now you must consider purchasing a picture from a professional photographer. There are thousands of pictures online to which you can buy the licensed right to publish. Try using Google or another search engine to look for "Royalty-free images." Prepare yourself to spend hours at this. You may find a picture on an entirely free site, however, your time is limited, so go ahead and look through the pictures on professional sites such as istockphoto.com, where you can buy a license for well under $100, perhaps as little as $30.

> Note: Prices vary as to picture size and the popularity of the photographer. The most I ever paid was $70. More on that later.

You will probably find several images that you wish to try out. This is quite all right; actually they expect you to try before you buy. Once you enter your business name and address, and choose a password, you may download a free sample for designing purposes. This will not be the quality of a purchased picture and it will have a trademark splashed across the front to prevent its use in a published design. It is understood that designers need to try-out several shots before choosing a final one to purchase. Some websites will have a command where you can "download a sample." Other times you can simply highlight, right-click and select a "save as" command. Sometimes you have to pull down a "tools" menu and select, "save as a picture."

Note: I recommend that you save these sample pictures in a separate "Sample Pictures" sub-folder in "My Pictures" file or "My Books" file. Also, re-title your saved picture so as to identify the website and file number of the picture in the "Save" title. Otherwise, you could spend hours trying to find the thing again, after you decided to buy it. In time, you will have a large number of samples in your Sample Pictures folder. You can keep these for later designing use, so long as you do not try to publish with them.

Later when you buy a picture, keep it in a file folder titled, "Licensed Pictures." Obviously you do not want to mix up the two.

Note: Royalty free does not mean entirely free. You still have to buy a license to use the picture in a publication. Royalty free means that you would not pay a royalty to the photographer for each and every book sold. A license does not give you an "exclusive right." That costs a lot more. Most picture sites will tell you how many other folks have purchased a license to use this particular picture.

Now that you have a folder of sample pictures, you can access these using the "From my computer" command in the "Cover Creator" web site in Kindle publishing.

Note: Before you try to do this, it will save time, if you know where on your computer you filed the pictures you want to use.

In the "Kindle eBook Cover Creator," in the "1 Choose Design" section or the "2 Style and Edit" section, click "Choose a new cover image," and then choose "From my computer."

A window opens up on your computer. Is this the correct location? If not, locate the correct file from the list on the left of your display, open the file folder and click or double click on this. In the correct file, scroll down to your desired picture, and select it. The title should appear in the "file name" address window at the very bottom of the page. If the correct file name has appeared, click "Open." The picture will jump into your cover creator display.

Shortcut: sometimes you merely have to double click on the correct picture to make it open in your cover.

Change your mind? Quickly try another by clicking "Choose a new cover image," "From my computer," and clicking and entering a new image.

The time will come when you have narrowed your choices down to two or three. This is good. Use your first choice, for now. You can always change your mind later. It is time to make a temporary design choice and move on. Click on one design.

Next we are going to select "2 Style and Edit." Here is where you can do amazing things with colors, fonts and sizes, and edit the picture.

However, by now, you are probably getting really tired. You are not finished, but you should save your progress before you exit and take a break.

While in "2 Style and Edit," click Save.

> Note: Do not click "Save and Submit" under "3 Preview" until you are actually ready to submit. More on that later.

Next, you can either use the back arrow to go back to your Book Detail page where you can Save as Draft, before you exit; or, you can simply click the window closed. When you return, next time to your eBook Detail page you will be able to "Launch Cover Creator," and continue with your design where you left off.

Working with "2 Style and Edit."

And now the fun begins. Here is where you cut loose your creative soul. You can change colors, fonts, sizes, and move things around to your heart's content.

Hover your mouse over the three icons near the bottom left. You will see:

- Choose Colors
- Choose layout
- Choose fonts

We will experiment with these choices. First, let us experiment with the pre-set color combinations for background, text and accent colors. Under "Choose Colors" the two categories are "Custom Colors" or "Select a Color Scheme."

First, try selecting a color scheme, one at a time, to see what happens. If you have covered your entire layout with a picture there will not be a background, so nothing will change, except the color of your text. However, if your picture covers only a portion of your design, there will be lots of changes in the background colors. See?

Next, we will go over to the "Custom Colors" side. Here you can go crazy with an entire palate of colors to choose among. Try changing, one by one, and see what happens.

> Note: Here is one place where I have to double-click, rather than single-click. Don't ask me why.

Next, select the icon for "Choose fonts." Here you will see a selection of pre-set font options. Try switching from one to another.

> Note: If you are working on a small computer, not all the choices will show on your display. Use the large arrows to move right and left. Choose one. You can always change your mind, later.

Note: Any time you decide to take a break, remember to Save at the bottom of this page. Frequent saves are good, you know.

So far, so good.

Working with Layout

We are still in the "2 Style and Edit" section. Click on the icon for "Choose a Layout." (Forget where that is? Bottom left--three icons. The middle one.) Easily click on the eight options, one at a time. Your text will pop around to various settings. It only takes a few seconds to see them all and choose one. You can change your mind later.

Before you move on to the next item, be sure and "Save."

Working with Design Elements

Ta-dah! You are going to be super creative. Have you saved? Good, because you may muddle everything up. We are going to get into the mud and mess around.

Perhaps, by now, you are getting close to your chosen book cover. But, before you quit, let us suppose that you want to change a single item in your design, without affecting the whole and without sticking with one of the preset designs.

Here is a trick:

You can click on any element in your design and highlight it for the purpose of changing it around.

Let's say you are not quite satisfied with the size of the picture you chose. Maybe it is confusing your text, or maybe you want more background color to show. Click near the edge of your design and "handles" will appear on your picture.

> Note: You may need to try a different spot before the picture's handles show up.

You can try "dragging" a handle to change the size and/or placement of the picture, in order to uncover some of the background color or design.

> (Note: Not all designs allow this.)

Likewise, you can click on the title to "select" it. A toolbar opens. Now you can change the size and the font from a whole host of available fonts. You can move it around, right, left, justified, change the color and do everything that you would normally do with fonts. (Tip: If nothing is happening, you probably need to highlight the word[s] or letter[s] you wish to affect.)

Another option is to change the author's font in a similar fashion.

If you should stumble onto something you really, really like, be sure and save.

Finally, click near the bottom of your design to work on the sub-title in a similar fashion.

> Note: Perhaps you did not designate a sub-title, on your eBook Details page. After you save, you can use your back

arrow to return to your eBook Content page, select Kindle eBook Details and add a sub-title. Then, return to Kindle eBook Content and select Launch Cover Creator. Make the choice between Old and New. Good job. You can always change your mind and delete it, later.

Working with "3 Preview"

Return to your cover design, using the "Launch Cover Creator" link, on your "eBook Content" page.

Select "3 Preview."

Notice the Preview Options, the Save and Submit button and the tiny magnifying glass. We will experiment with these options, to see what happens.

By default you will be in Color Mode. You can select Gray Scale or Thumbnail. Your design should read easily in each of these modes.

Try the magnifying glass. As you know, Amazon has a "Read Inside" feature that magnifies the cover.

Note: The magnified version will demonstrate whether your picture has enough dots per inch. More on that later.

To exit out of this mode, simply click or double-click in a blank area of your display.

Preview your cover in all the options. Are you satisfied? If not, feel free to return to design area 1 or 2 and fix things.

After fixing, return to "3. Preview" and check it out, once again. Continue these steps until you are happy with your cover. In a moment we are going to Save and Submit, but first...

Put your design in color mode and (Option: enlage it byusing the magnifying icon.) and right click. Select "Save Image As." Notice the title is a long string of gobble-de-goop. Erase that and change the title to something you will remember such as "My [enter book title] eCover #1." Before you click Save, look at the address. You probably want to change that, as well, to something like this:

MyComputer/MyDocuments/MyBooks.

> Note: Be sure you understand where you have saved the cover, so you can find it later on your computer. It is good to have a special place for all your covers.

You can also save it on a Memory Stick, Flash Drive, desktop, or in several places. Now is a good time to get organized, so that everything about this book is in one place on your computer, as well as on a backup drive.

> Note: Now you might to print your cover with your own printer. However, you can

also print it later from your computer file. If you do not see a print option right away, do this: Right click picture to open a menu. Select "open image in new tab." Now you should see a print option.

Next: Go to thumbnail mode and save your thumbnail in the same place on your computer. This time, title it something like this: My [Book Title] Cover #1 thumbnail.

> Note: Always title each subsequent version with the same title #2, #3 and so on. It is a good idea to delete all the old versions, once in a while. They will be sent to your trash can. Remember you can always recover a trashcan file until the day when you empty the trash, once and for all.

Advanced Tip: Here is a trick: Commandeer a friend for this test.

Prop needed: One color printed copy of your book cover, full sized, on 8.5 X 11 paper, or 8.5 X 14 paper.

While hiding the picture, position yourself well across the room from your friend. Instruct your friend to "Please close your eyes." Now, hold the picture for the friend to see, and say, "Now open your eyes and look at the picture, please." Allow only a few seconds look-see, enough for a first impression, because that is all your customer will get. Hide the picture again. Ask your friend, "What did you see first?" and then, "What did you see second?" and then, "Did you see anything else?"

An observant person will tell you where their eyes focused first, second and third. This will inform you whether the customer sees your most important element first, and so on.

Your can repeat the test, with the understanding that there is only one "first" impression. You can even do this test on yourself, after a few hours away from the picture. It is best if the most important item pops out first and leads the eye directly to the second item.

Advanced tip: For example: let us say you have a picture of a person looking off to the side. Please have the person's eyes directed toward the book title, not away from it. You may need to reposition the picture or "flip" it, using your picture tool bar.

Example 2: Let us suppose your picture has a "tunnel" effect, perhaps a line of trees or a highway leading off into the distance. Ask yourself, "Where does the picture lead the eye?" Toward the end of the tunnel, right? So, obviously, place your title there, or just above that spot.

Save and Submit

Are you satisfied with your cover? Ask yourself: Does it give the customer a clue as to what is inside? Does the title show up in thumbnail size? Does it scream "Look at me?" How about the author's name? Does it show? If not, decide whether that is necessary. The thumbnail needs to show only one or two important elements.

> Note: Amazon will display the title and author alongside the thumbnail.

Maybe you are close enough for now. If so, now is the time to click "Save and Submit" from the "3 Preview" page. Your cover will show up in the thumbnail size on your "Kindle eBook Content" page. If all your other elements are finished, you may now click "Save and Continue" at the bottom of this page.

Page three, "Kindle eBook Pricing", will show up, where you answer a few questions, agree to terms, and state that you own the rights to this manuscript. Click submit and your baby will zoom off to the Amazon Kindle editors for review. During this anxious waiting period, you cannot make changes to the cover, or the interior, for that matter.

In a few hours, or days, you will receive an email telling you whether they have accepted your design, or not. If not, they will tell you what needs to be fixed. Sometimes they will accept it with some comments or reservations. The most likely one being, "Your image is less than the recommended 300 dpi. It may not display effectively."

Well, let us suppose it shows up a little blurry in the life-size version. You may decide that blurry is exactly what you want. In that case, ignore their advice. (Note: See the cover of this book, for example.) However, if you want it to appear sharp in any size, you may have to go back and buy a larger, more-costly version of your picture, at some point in time. More on that later.

Buying a License for a Picture

If you decide to use a purchased image, you can wait until almost the end to invest the money in a license.

> Note: Do not make the mistake of using a copyrighted picture without paying for the license. It is not worth the risk.

On your computer, go to the sample pictures file where you remember you have stored your sample pictures. Maybe you cannot be sure which one it is. Here is a tip:

Tip: If your document list does not show the actual picture, look up in the top right of your display. Hesitate your mouse over the tiny icons until you find one that says "Change your view." Click on the tiny down arrow just to the right of the rectangular icon and pull down a menu with eight items. Choose "extra large icons." Now you will be able to scroll through the available pictures until you find the exact one you need.

When you find it, write down, copy, or remember the name of the web site and the file number of the picture.

(Remember I recommended you save that, earlier? Aren't you glad you did? I once spent a day looking for a lost picture I had chosen. You see all the trouble I have saved you? Ahem. Give yourself a pat on the back.)

Now you can go to the correct web site and search for the exact picture by number. Click on the picture and examine the bewildering options and prices available. Depending on the finished size you will need, you must purchase a size that will display at close to 300 dpi or more. (Less will be somewhat blurry.) Let us suppose that a 5 X 7, dpi 300, choice is $30 and an 8 X 10, dpi 300, is $60. Think: What is the largest size I need? Probably no more than 5 X 7 would fill your entire book cover. However, if you are reducing the size to half a page, a smaller size will do, so long as it works out to 300 dpi or more.

> Tip: If you buy a smaller size and then use your picture editing tool to stretch it to cover a larger area, the dpi will reduce, accordingly. Dpi stands for "dots per [square] inch." Logically, if you spread 300 dots from one inch to two, both ways, the dots must cover four square inches instead of one. Do the math... 300/4=75 dpi. Ouch–way too blurry. The same principle works in reverse, if you make a picture smaller, the dots will concentrate and become denser, thus, sharper in detail.

For your purposes, you do not need to be exact. You can estimate the size you need and use the old "trial and error" method to see what works. Remember you are creating an eBook cover. A computer screen can only show so much detail, so buy the cheapest one that gets by. When in doubt, buy the less costly one (not necessarily the very cheapest). Why? Because most sites will allow you to trade up, but not trade down. Check it out before you buy. You can probably trade-in your purchase on a larger size of the same image and pay the difference in price, within a reasonable time period.

Once you have purchased your image and stored it in your "Licensed Pictures" folder, you can use it more than once, in different ways and different modes. You may want to edit it. Try cropping out the parts you do not want. Try putting it into an oval or other shape, blurring the edges, changing the colors, and more endless changes. Perhaps you want to put the full color picture on the front cover, and use a grayscale cropped picture inside your book. Use the picture or forms of the picture in your ads, emails, catalogs, and Facebook pages. Likewise you can use the full cover in as many ways as your imagination permits.

Note: Simple picture editing tools are available in Microsoft Word. Merely double-click a picture and the editing toolbar will pop up. (Sometimes you have to go up to the Format section of your toolbar and click Format Picture.) There are more complex tools on your computer, available from the Picture gallery. However, I have found that the tools in Microsoft Word are easy, fast, and suitable for most purposes.

Tip: Remember to "Save-As" your picture(s) in jpeg, or jpg, format, as this is the one that is required for most purposes.

Note: You can quickly change the size. Click on the picture to create "handles."

Drag a corner handle to change the size without changing the proportions. Drag a side handle to change proportions.

Tip: After editing a picture, use the "Save As" command to save the new version. Give it an appropriate title and number and save it in your Pictures file, and/or My Books file, wherever you have the original. When you close out of this version, the original may still be there. When you close out of the original version, it will ask you if you want to Save. I recommend that you *do not* save the changes, as you have already done so. Also, you want to preserve the original. Simply close without saving. (I know this is scary.) Now you have both versions saved in the same place.

`*` *`*`* *`*`* *`*`*

Dear Reader.

Was this booklet helpful to you? Did it deliver as promised? If you liked it, please do me a favor and leave a comment or question <u>here:</u> http://www.mercerpublications.com/guestbook.html

We love to hear from you and promise to answer your question, if at all possible.

Click or go here for a free bonus eBook:

http://www.mercerpublications.com/freegiftebook.html

Help us out: More online opportunities:

- Please go to your country's Amazon Marketplace and leave a simple, but nice, five-star review.
- Simply enter Dorothy May Mercer into the Search area and click Go. All seven pages of our books will pop up.
- Thanks a million

(Not many folks will take the trouble to post a review, and even fewer will bother to copy and paste it in other marketplaces. You are truly one in ten million!)

- If you purchased this book, I know you will not "return" it for a refund. Sometimes, customers do so, perhaps unaware that it puts a black mark on the author's record. Amazon keeps track of these things.
- If you used the Amazon library option, and borrowed this book, you may return it,

now, and borrow it again, anytime. You may even buy it. Whee!

While you are there, please consider buying/borrowing another book by Dorothy May Mercer. Or, you may consider the Want-to-buy option and put several books on your "Add to Wish List." Amazon notices everything! Besides, this list makes a good suggestion list for your next birthday or anniversary. Your relatives and friends will thank you.

Another good option is the "Give as a Gift." Amazon sends a beautiful gift card to the recipient. You can add your own special message. Easy-Peezy.

Two easy ways to find all of the Dorothy May Mercer books:

1. Go to www.MercerPublications.com for links.

   Tip: Look at the "How to For You" menu for 23 helpful books for authors and indie publishers.

2. Go to any Amazon site and search for Dorothy May Mercer.

   Tip: There is more than one Amazon page for her books. The control at the bottom of the first page will navigate you to any page of her books.

Links to all of these books can be found at www.mercerpublications.com

The complete "How to For You" series of booklets for improving writers and Indie Publishers.

1. "How to Write Sentences and Paragraphs" *in Your Novel*
2. "How to Install a Link in Your Document"
3. "How to Sell Your eBook Using Amazon Free Days"
4. "How to Prepare Your Book for Kindle"
5. "How to Fix Errors in Your Document," *Find and Replace Globally*
6. "How to Use Your Book for Free Ads"
7. "How to Design and Format Your Paragraphs"
8. "How to Design a Kindle eBook Cover"

9. "How to Install Your Kindle Cover on Print Books," *and Vice Versa*

10. "How to Add an Interactive Table of Contents"

11. "How to Format Your Book, for Publishing"—*Two Editions, Ebook and Print*

12. "How to Edit a Book," With a Friend—*Two Editions, Ebook and Print*

13. "How to Write Great Dialog"—*Two Editions, Ebook and Print*

14. "How to Market Your Book," Marketing 101—*Two Editions, Ebook and Print*

15. "Book Covers Bargain Bundle," Two for One, Includes #8 and #9-- *Print Edition Only*

16. "Marketing Bargain Bundle," Two for One, Includes #14 and #6-- *Print Edition Only*

17. "Book Marketing Bargain Bundle," Three for One, Includes #14, #6 and # 3-*Print Edition Only*

18. "Formatting Bargain Bundle," Two for One, Includes # 7 and # 11- *Print Edition Only*

19. "How to Register ISBNs & Copyrights" *– Two Editions, Ebook and Print*

20. "How to Get an Audible Version'" *for Your Book– Two Editions, Ebook and Print*

21. "How to Self-Publish" *Your Book– Two Editions, Ebook and Print* (Includes #11 and #20)

22. "How to Write Fiction" *– Two Editions, Ebook and Print*

23. "How to Create a Picture Book" – *Two Editions, Ebook and Print*

Links to all of these books can be found at www.mercerpublications.com

BOOKS FROM MERCER PUBLICATIONS

Links to all of these books can be found at www.mercerpublications.com

All novels are page-turners, complete stories in themselves.

- **The McBride Series of Action Novels, Starring Det. Lt. Michael J. McBride Jr.**

available in English and Spanish, ebook, print and Audible editions

"Car oo6 Responding" Busy border cops. Mike meets Juli

."The Cocaine Chase" Drug king-pin escapes again.

"The Golden Coin" Illegal immigrants collide with violent cartels.

"The Cartel Wars" break out in the US. Mike proposes Juli.

"The Gang Bust" Wrap-up gangs & drug criminals. M & J wed.

Same as above in Spanish

"Unidad oo6 Respondiendo"

"La Casa di la Cocaina"

"El Immigrant e la Monada Dorada

"La Guerras Cartel"

"La Pandilla Busto

- **The Washington McBride Novels, Starring Senator Mike McBride, his wife Juliette, featuring his bodyguard, Cynthia Patterson. available in ebook, print and Audible editions**

"the Fairfax Fix" Based on true story. H.S. girls recruited into prostitution ring. 4 disappear. Cops invstigate.

"the Arlington Alias" Investigative reporter, Juli McBride, exposes D.C. human trafficking ring.

s"the Savage Surrogate" Fran is kidnapped into slavery as surrogate mom. Juli searches world for her.

- **The McBride Suspense/Romances, available in eBook, print and Audible editions**

"Fran and Max" The Bungalow. Pregnant and hidden from the syndicate. Will they find her?

"Cynthia and Dan," Cyber War. Terrorists attempt assassinate Pres with drones. "C" falls mysterious stranger.

"Mary Beth and Sammy," Rolling Thunder. Dumb college kid joins gangs. Co-ed disappears. MB falls for handsome guy.

"Nate" The Search Father's search for long-lost daughter. Terrorists plot hi-tech multiple plane crashes.

"E-M-P Honeymoon" New bride blunders into terrorists plot. Can CIA & US Space Force save her?

Photo-Travel books by Dorothy May Mercer, author, and Dave Mercer, photographer:

- o "Alaska and Back" With Dave and Dorothy.
- o "Africa and Back" With Dave and Dorothy
- o "Hawaii and Back," Vol. 1 Kauai" With Dave and Dorothy
- o "Hawaii and Back," Vol 2, Maui, With Dave and Dorothy
- o "Hawaii and Back," Vol 3, Oahu, With Dave and Dorothy
- o "Hawaii and Back," Vol 4, Kauai Via SFO, With Dave and Dorothy
- o "Niagara and Back," With Dave and Dorothy

More books by Dorothy May Mercer:

"Leon and Esther," an historical Christian love story. Perfect for the Advent season, or anytime.

"Stories I Haven't Told," an auto-biography. Barefoot Depression baby becomes multi-millionaire CEO.

Various Author's Books published by Mercer Publications & Ministries, Inc.:

- o "Let's Talk" a Black/White Dialog in the US & the UK

- "Short & Fun Stories" Vol. 1 & 2, by fourteen authors.
- "Stormy Affair," a Romance, by Netty Ejike
- "Sensual Bond," 5 Part Saga Series, by Netty Ejike
- "He Called Her Hat," That Tough Little Lady, Amusing Historical Biography, by Myron C. McDonald
- "Notes from John," Messages from Beyond, by Marcia McMahon
- "Remember How Much I Love You," Romantic Action Suspense, by Dale L. Williams, M.D.
- "The Inheritance from Hell," True Drama, by R.D. Margot
- "Ascension Teachings," With Archangel Michael, by Marcia McMahon
- "Gems" a collection of dream-time peotry, by Nancy Calumet, illustrated by Dorothy May Mercer
- "Without from Within" a poetry collection, by Ron Shaw

New in Audible Book (Talking Books) Versions:

The McBride Series of Action Novels, Starring Det. Lt. Michael J. McBride Jr. in English & Spanish Audible version:

"Car 006 Responding"

"The Cocaine Chase"

"The Golden Coin"

"The Cartel Wars

"The Gang Bust"

Action Novels in Audible version:

"The Fairfax Fix"

"The Arlington Alias"

"The Savage Surrogate"

Action/Romantic Suspense Novels in Audible versions:

"Fran and Max, The Bungalow

"Cynthia and Dan" *Cyber War*

"Mary Beth and Sammy," *Rolling Thunder*

"Leon and Esther"

"E-M-P Honeymoon" Kelly & Tom

Non-Fiction in Audible version:"

"Let's Talk" a Black/White Dialog in the US & the UK

In return, a bonus gift for you, just for reading this book.

PLEASE Continue on for a Bonus Bargain Book.

Go to MercerPublications.com and scroll down to Short & Fun Stories:

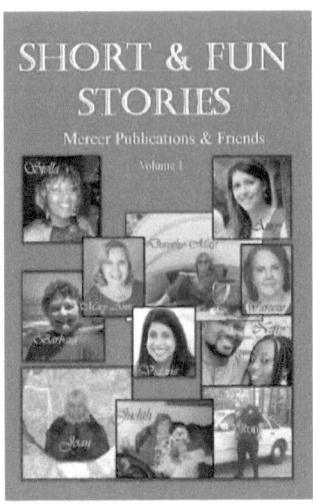

For a wonderful free E book from MercerPublications.com click on the title, "Short & Fun Stories," enter your email address and click Send.

And while you are enjoying a fun read, please order another book or booklet by these authors.

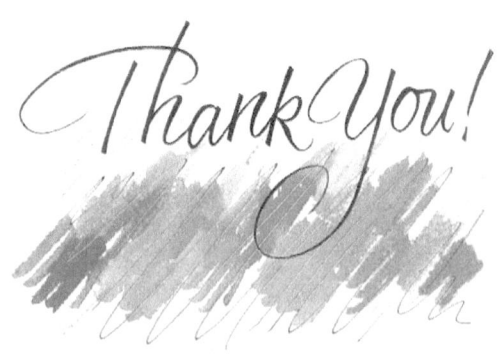

Dorothy May Mercer, Author Extraordinaire